THE BABYSITTER'S HANDBOOK

BY K. D. KUCH
ILLUSTRATED BY J. J. SMITH-MOORE

Medical information reviewed by
Gale Lawrence, M.D., family physician

RANDOM HOUSE NEW YORK

To Michael, my number-one babysitter

http://www.randomhouse.com/

Library of Congress Cataloging-in-Publication Data:
Kuch, Kayte.
The babysitter's handbook / by K. D. Kuch ; illustrated by J. J. Smith-Moore.
p. cm. — (KidBacks) ISBN 0-679-88369-X [1. Babysitting—Handbooks, manuals,
etc.—Juvenile literature.] I. Smith-Moore, J. J., 1955— ill. II. Title. III. Series.
HQ769.5.K83 1997 649'.1'0248—dc20 96-34428

Printed in the United States of America 10 9 8 7 6 5 4 3 2 1

KIDBACKS is a trademark of Random House, Inc.

CONTENTS

•••••••••••••••• ⚗ ••••••••••••••••

BECOMING A BABYSITTER

• • • • • • • • • • • • • • ⚬ • • • • • • • • • • • • •

Are you looking for something fun to do after school or on weekends? In need of a little extra cash? Do you like playing games, singing, and reading books? If you answered yes to these questions, then babysitting may be the job for you!

Babysitting is a great way for girls and boys to have a positive influence on a child and earn money. You can form lasting relationships with children that become an important part of your life.

Babysitting is a very rewarding job, but it takes a responsible individual to do it well. Babysitting requires more than just "watching" children. You have to be able to feed, clothe, and play with the children in your care, as well as keep them safe.

If you've wanted to be a babysitter for a long time, or if you've just started thinking about it, this book will give you important information on getting started.

For those of you who have already started babysitting, this book is filled with new ideas for entertaining children, along with helpful hints to make your job easier and lots more fun.

NOTE FROM THE AUTHOR

While there are a few suggestions on taking care of babies, the focus of *The Babysitter's Handbook* is on babysitting toddlers and older children.

If you're a first-time babysitter, it's best to gain experience with older children, before taking care of infants. After several babysitting jobs, if you feel you are ready to look after babies, it's important to take a class that offers information on babysitting infants to help you feel prepared and confident. (You'll find out all about babysitter courses on page 8.)

GETTING DOWN TO BUSINESS

Becoming a babysitter is a big responsibility. There are several aspects to this job that deserve serious thought. A babysitter needs to handle almost everything that a parent would normally take care of. Although this job can be a lot of fun, it should never be taken lightly. Children depend on their babysitters to care for them while their parents are away. If you mean business and want to become a great babysitter, here are a few questions to ask yourself before you begin your career in child care:

- **Do I really like kids?**
One of the first things you want to ask yourself is how you feel about children. If the idea of being around kids doesn't sound like fun, maybe you should think about getting a job with adults. Perhaps you would prefer volunteering at a hospital or a nursing home. It could be that you love children but don't feel ready to handle tiny babies. That's okay—you can target an age group, like toddlers or middle-graders. This is your own business—so it's up to you.

- **How will my job affect my family?** It's always important to talk to your family before starting a job. You probably have responsibilities around your house, too, so discuss with your family how much time you can allot to your babysitting business. And talk to them about what you'll need from them. You may need a family member to drop you off and pick you up from your job. And you may want one of them to be available to call in case of an emergency.

- **How often can I babysit?** Babysitting can fit into almost any schedule. Figure out what times are best for you, such as after school, evenings, or weekends. Don't forget to factor in any other activities that require your participation. Your babysitting career should never get in the way of your school-work. Chances are you will be too busy watching the kids and playing with them to cram for a test or do your homework.

- **Am I old enough?** There are no national guidelines about how old you have to be to babysit. It depends on a lot of factors, including what your family says, how the people hiring

---

THE TOP 10 LIST
What Parents Want in a Babysitter

Here's what parents are looking for when they hire a babysitter:

1. Responsibility
2. A genuine interest in their child
3. Sensitivity to their child's needs
4. Honesty
5. Punctuality
6. Kindness and gentleness, but firmness when needed
7. Respect for parents' privacy and possessions
8. Ability to be focused and calm on the job
9. Common sense
10. Friendliness

SMART SITTER TIP #1
GO TO THE HEAD OF THE CLASS

It's important to begin your babysitting career with the necessary knowledge and skills to do a good job. Check around your community to find classes offered in infant and child care, safety, first aid, and lifesaving techniques. You might also find classes geared especially for first-time babysitters. These classes are taught by medical and safety professionals in your community. They will provide you with information, answer your questions, and give you a chance to practice what you learn. Most classes are held over a period of six to eight sessions. Most require you to take a test before you receive a certificate of completion. That will give prospective clients peace of mind and let them know you take your babysitting job very seriously.

For classes in your neighborhood, check with hospitals, churches, community centers, parks and recreation departments, or your local YMCA, YWCA, or chapter of the American Red Cross. Also, you may want to contact these national organizations for information about programs that might be available in your community.

SAFE SITTER
1500 North Ritter Avenue
Indianapolis, IN 46219
(800) 255-4089

Safe Sitter is a program used by many hospital and community groups to teach babysitting basics and rescue techniques to boys and girls from eleven to thirteen years old.

AMERICAN RED CROSS
NATIONAL HEADQUARTERS
431 18th Street, NW
Washington, DC 20006
(202) 737-8300

American Red Cross has chapters in most communities. They offer a variety of classes on infant and child care, as well as rescue techniques.

CAMPFIRE BOYS AND GIRLS
4601 Madison Avenue
Kansas City, MO 64112
(816) 756-1950

Campfire Boys and Girls offer a beginning babysitting class. They also offer a special course on taking care of developmentally delayed and disabled youngsters.

you feel, and how comfortable you feel handling this job. Have you ever been on your own while your parents were away? If the answer is no, you may need a little more time. But if you've been responsible for younger brothers and sisters, then you already have a head start to a successful babysitting career.

My Favorite Babysitter

"Danielle is my favorite sitter. She comes from a big family, which may be the reason she doesn't panic easily. She has a good head on her shoulders and handles the boys effortlessly. And they like her, too!"

Kathy, mother of two boys
Providence, Rhode Island

- **Can I handle an emergency?** Do you know what to do in an emergency? If you're going to take responsibility for someone else's children, you need to know. The best way to learn what to do in an emergency is to think about it before you begin babysitting. This book will introduce you to important safety information. It's a good idea to try to take classes in child care, first aid, and lifesaving procedures. Knowing this information and practicing safety techniques will help you feel confident and secure that you are prepared for every job.

IT PAYS TO ADVERTISE

Once you've made the decision to start your babysitting business, you need to think about the next step—how to get some customers! Don't worry—it's not hard! Just think of your favorite music store. You've probably seen their ads in the newspaper or on TV. And you may have heard one of your friends say they had a great selection of new CDs. The music store's advertisements (and your friend's recommendation) gave you information that made you want to visit the store. The same goes for your services as a babysitter. You've got to let people know that you're available and that you are a qualified babysitter for their kids. Here's how you can start:

Make an Ad

Get creative and design an advertisement for yourself. On a plain piece of paper, write a headline across the top, such as RESPONSIBLE BABYSITTER or BABYSITTER AVAILABLE. Then add a few lines about why a parent would want to hire you (see example on the opposite page).

✔ Add your target age group and whether you have any experience with babies or toddlers.
✔ Put together a list of references (learn how on page 14). Then, in the ad, include the line "REFERENCES UPON REQUEST" for those people who are interested.
✔ Put down the times you're available to babysit.
✔ The most important piece of information you can include is any babysitting or first aid classes you've completed.

You can make your ad more eye-catching by adding a little artwork. It can be a drawing, a photograph, or simply a fancy border that sets off your words. You can use a computer to help you design your ad or your own artistic skills! Always remember to print neatly and make sure your spelling is correct. (For safety reasons, you should not include your home address on the ad.)

How and Where to Advertise

Now that you have your flyer, it's time to spread the word. Have copies made at your local print shop (try colored paper). Then pass out the ad in your neighborhood to families you know who have young children. To give a possible client the best first impression, don't just leave the flyer on the porch or under the door:

BABYSITTER AVAILABLE

Fourteen-year-old girl

- Experience with infants and toddlers

- Has taken CPR and babysitters' courses

- Available after school, evenings, and weekends

- References upon request

Call Kari 555-1234

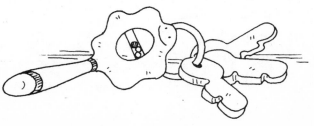

knock on the door and give it to the mother or father personally. If your church or synagogue has a community bulletin board, ask if you can post it there. Only hang your ad in familiar areas.

Word of Mouth Is the Best

Tell your parents, friends, relatives, and neighbors that you are free to babysit. Ask them to pass the word around. You never know when your best friend's next-door neighbor's niece might need a babysitter!

My Favorite Babysitter

"I found my favorite sitter through a friend of a friend. This thirteen-year-old boy had created a great reputation for himself, and the word about him spread all over the neighborhood!"

Sam, father of two sons
Downey, California

GETTING THE JOB

Getting your phone to ring is only one step to finding your first babysitting job. The next step is to be hired. New customers are going to have some questions for you. If you think about those questions beforehand, you can be prepared with terrific answers that will help calm nervous parents and convince them of your reliability. Some things parents might ask about include your age, your experience level, and whether you have had first aid training. Read on for some ideas about putting your best foot forward.

Be Businesslike

Handle the business aspects of babysitting in a professional and confident manner. Even little things make big impressions!

✔ *Always* be polite and courteous on the phone.

✔ Have a notebook to write down all important babysitting information.

✔ When you have a job, call the day before to confirm.

✔ Don't hesitate to ask *any* questions.

✔ Don't be afraid to discuss babysitting rates. It's always best to work out your fees up front so there are no surprises for your clients or you. (Read more about money matters on page 15.)

CHECKLIST FOR A NEW FAMILY

Here are some preliminary questions you will need to ask to help you prepare for your job with a new family.

1. How did the family get your name?

2. What is their address and phone number?

3. What are the names and ages of the children you will be sitting for?

4. Are there any special circumstances (like a child with an illness or disability)?

5. Is your babysitting fee acceptable to them?

6. Will they pick you up and take you home?

7. What are the date and times they will need you?

SMART SITTER TIP #2
WHEN YOU NEED TO SAY NO

If you decide not to babysit for a family—or an emergency comes up and you have to cancel—make sure to call the family immediately. It's important to give them enough time to find another babysitter.

SMART SITTER TIP #3
WRITE IT DOWN

It's essential to stay on top of your schedule. Remember to use a calendar to avoid scheduling two babysitting jobs for the same night, or arriving at the wrong time. Any style will do, as long as you have enough space to write down the information pertaining to the appointment. Always keep your notebook handy. The best place is probably near the telephone.

As soon as you make a new appointment, write it down. If you put it off until later, you may forget. Remember to include other meaningful dates as well— music lessons, vacations, that dreaded trip to the dentist!

Prepare a List of References

A parent you haven't worked for before might ask for your references. That's just a list of people who know you and can vouch for your character. The best people to use as references are people you have worked for in the past. If you don't have any work experience, a minister, rabbi, teacher, or neighbor who knows you

WHAT SMART SITTERS SAY

"It's sort of funny now, but I once really messed up a babysitting appointment. It happened around the time my sister, Debbie, was planning her wedding. One night I was helping her write out the invitations when I got a phone call from a new family. They wanted me to sit for their two-year-old on Saturday night. I didn't write it down. That was my mistake. I arrived on Saturday, but it was a week too early!"

Angie G., age 15, Redmond, Washington

well makes a good reference. Before you're even asked, prepare a list of references. Make sure to include names, phone numbers, and the relationship you have with these people (employer/ employee, minister/church member, teacher/student). Before you make up the list, ask each person if you can include him or her as a reference.

Arrange for a Pre-visit

It's always a good idea to meet the child and family before you begin working for them, and to become familiar with the house and neighborhood. Ask an adult member of your family to go with you, so *your* family feels comfortable with the arrangement as well. Remember to bring along a notebook and write every- thing down—special instructions for the kids as well as emer- gency information and phone numbers. Next, use the time to get to know the child. This will help the child to feel more comfort- able when you show up to babysit.

WHAT SMART SITTERS SAY

"At first I was embarrassed when my dad wanted to meet the family I was going to sit for. But it worked out okay. They didn't mind at all."

Leigh, age 13, Bloomington, Minnesota

MONEY MATTERS

There is no set rate for babysitters. Sometimes it depends on what part of the country you live in. In large cities, you might get more money. If a parent has used other babysitters recently, he or she might have a rate in mind. Sometimes it depends on how much experience you have. Other times, how many kids you are going to watch will factor into the fee. New parents may not know what to pay, so it's up to you to decide what your average rate will be.

Setting Your Babysitting Fee

Before you can set your fee, you need to do some investigating. Ask your friends who are babysitters what they usually charge, or what their older brothers and sisters charge. Then ask your parents and their friends what they pay sitters. You'll find that older, experienced babysitters charge more. New babysitters tend to earn a little less. Some sitters get more money for staying past midnight, staying overnight, taking care of more than one child, or doing extra chores. Once you've gotten all this information, you can decide what is the appropriate rate for you to charge.

My Favorite Babysitter

"Once I hired a babysitter who asked for one dollar an hour more than I was used to paying. She explained that she was trying to pay for the babysitting class she had taken at the parks and recreation department. Since I knew she had that good training, the extra money was worth it."

Diane, mother of three daughters
Chicago, Illinois

WHAT SMART SITTERS SAY

"I have a base price for one child. I charge double for two. If there are more than that, I charge an extra fifty cents an hour per child. But I sometimes charge less for my regular customers."

Nick, age 14, Bridgeport, Connecticut

Smart Sitter Tip #4
KEEP A RECORD

If you have a lot of clients and you charge them different rates depending on what they require of you, things might get confusing and embarrassing. Keep a little notebook with the charges. You can also record clients' addresses, phone numbers, the names of their children, and any other important information, such as "Kate likes fairy tales and Pete likes board games."

Talking Money

Surprising as it may seem, even adults have a hard time talking about money with potential customers or current bosses. But it's important you get that part of the business out of the way as soon as possible. That means the first time a parent calls. Talk about your rates up front to avoid surprises at the end of the babysitting job. If you feel too uncomfortable, or you are afraid you'll say the wrong thing, then write a script for yourself. It doesn't have to be elaborate, just something simple, like: *"I charge x dollars an hour for one child and x dollars for two or more."*
If some parents think you're charging too much, you may have to explain how you arrived at your rates (it's the going rate for your neighborhood, or you have a lot of experience). If the parents still feel your rate is too high, you must decide to either hold your ground and pass up the job or lower your rate.

MORE THAN BABYSITTING

There's no official job description for a babysitter. But it's generally accepted that your main—and sometimes only—responsibility is to look after the kids. As part of your job you may also be expected to:

- Fix meals for the kids. Make sure you find out what they can or cannot eat. Wash any dishes you've used for the children and yourself. Remember to wipe off counters.

- Get kids ready for bed.

- Keep the house as organized as possible by putting toys and games away after use.

If you decide you want to take on additional tasks—like laundry, vacuuming, or raking the leaves—remember to discuss this with the parents first. These extra jobs should *never* distract you from the most important part of your job—the children. Some parents may want you to keep your focus only on their kids.

BABYSITTING BASICS

Once you get your first babysitting job, the real work begins. It's important that you start off on the right foot. This chapter is filled with ideas. Some are hard-and-fast rules you should always follow. Others are just suggestions. Remember, no two babysitters are alike. As you gain more experience, you will decide what babysitting basics work for you.

ARRIVE EARLY

In making arrangements with the family, suggest that you'd like to arrive at least fifteen minutes early. You'll need the time to go over any details. Remember, the more information you have, the more comfortable you will feel.

When you arrive, the parents might be a little harried getting ready. And they probably have some concern about leaving their children with someone new. The best thing you can do is greet them with a smile. When they're finished getting ready, take out your list of questions (see page 79). This will help reassure them.

Get Instructions

First on your list will be filling out the Emergency Card (see page 21). Get the number

---

My Favorite Babysitter

"Jimmy has to be my favorite babysitter, hands down. The first time he came over, he had a list of questions. Some things I hadn't even thought to tell him about, like where my earthquake supplies were."

Fran, mother of a girl and a boy
San Diego, California

where the parents can be reached and emergency numbers. Then remember to get the parents' instructions on the following:

- ✔ Feeding the kids
- ✔ Toileting/changing diapers (if needed)
- ✔ Bedtime
- ✔ Handling the phone or visitors
- ✔ Entertainment for kids
- ✔ Off-limits areas of the house
- ✔ Medicine (If the parents ask you to give medicine to a child, ask them to pre-measure or write down explicit instructions.)

Learn Where Things Are

If you haven't been to the house before, it's a good idea to ask for a tour. It's important that you know where to find the children's rooms, their toys, off-limits areas, and first aid supplies, as well as where the light switches and exits are. You'll also want to know how to work the heating and cooling systems. Take a moment to learn how the door and window locks work. Don't forget to ask about any security and fire alarms. You may never have to use them, but it's important to know what to do in case they go off. Ask if the family has an emergency evacuation plan. That's a designated area where the family will meet in case of a fire or other emergency in the house.

WHAT SMART SITTERS SAY

"I've only had to call the parents once. I thought the baby I was watching had swallowed a button. Fortunately, I found it just as the parents got home. But it's always better to be safe than sorry!"

Wendy, age 14, Clear Lake, Texas

EMERGENCY CARD

Fill out as much information as you can on a separate note card, then write in the rest of the information when you get to your job. Keep this card by the phone at your client's house at all times while you're sitting, in case  you need it quickly. After the job, take it home and use it again when you babysit for the same family. (Remember to check each time to see if any of the numbers have changed.) You should have an emergency card for each of your clients. You can store them in an old recipe file box.

EMERGENCY CARD

Family's name: _____ *(list first and last names)* _____

Address: _____ *(add nearest cross street)* _____

Phone number: _____ *(area code if it's different from yours)* ___

Burglar alarm code: _____

Emergency phone numbers:

Number where parents can be reached: _____

  Emergency numbers, if other than 911:

    police: _____

    fire: _____

  Emergency Medical Service (EMS)

    ambulance: _____

  Poison Control Center: _____

  Neighbors or other

    backup adult helpers: _____

    _____

SMART SITTER TIP #5
BEFORE YOU LEAVE HOME

Just as your clients leave the number for where they'll be, remember to leave information for your family, too! This includes the name, address, and phone number of the family you're sitting for. Also, write down the time you'll be leaving and the estimated time you'll be coming home. Put all the information where your family can find it, such as on the refrigerator or next to the phone.

MEETING THE KIDS

It's the big moment. You're about to ring the doorbell and meet the children you will be taking care of. Don't expect all little children to welcome you with open arms. In fact, you might be greeted by tears, or maybe even screams. That's understandable. Even little ones can sense that if you're there, that can only mean one thing—their parents are leaving them with someone they don't really know. Here are some great ways to break the ice and help make them feel comfortable.

1. **Go slow.** When you meet new kids, remember to give them time to warm up to you—especially younger children. You might want to tell them you're there to play with them.

WHAT SMART SITTERS SAY

"I always ask the parents what their child likes. One little boy I sit for likes the fish in the aquarium, so when his mom gets ready to leave, I take him over to watch the fish."

Brittany, age 15, Atlanta, Georgia

2. **Be interested in their world.** Start playing with one of the child's toys. Act casual and interested in it. The child may come over and take the toy away from you, but you've made contact and that's a start. The child might even come over and join you in play.

3. **Make them feel grown-up.** Ask them to show you how something works, like one of their toys. Or ask them to show you their room.

BYE-BYE TIME

The moment finally comes that all babysitters, parents, and little kids dread. The parents leave. It doesn't matter how incredible a babysitter you are—chances are the child will be upset. It's only natural. The child may cry, pound at the door, or sulk in a corner. Sometimes the crying stops five seconds after the parents leave. No problem, then. But what if it doesn't? Here's what to do:

WHAT TO WEAR WHILE YOU'RE BABYSITTING

It's important to arrive looking neat and presentable. But don't forget comfort! You'll probably be spending a lot of time bending, kneeling, squatting, and rolling around on the floor with kids. Your best bet is to wear comfortable and washable clothes. Blue jeans or shorts, T-shirts, and sneakers are always great choices. If you love wearing jewelry, remember that it can be dangerous for you and the children. Little kids love to pull on necklaces and earrings—so you might want to leave them home. Avoid wearing sharp pins as well.

- The best way to calm a child is with distraction. Pick up a toy and try to entice the child to play with you. You could also try coloring—drawing pictures or writing the child's name in bubble letters often gets their attention.

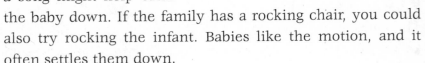

- For babies, anything that makes noise is a good diversion. A rattle, a squeaky toy, or singing a song might help calm the baby down. If the family has a rocking chair, you could also try rocking the infant. Babies like the motion, and it often settles them down.

If nothing seems to work, try not to get upset. Remember not to yell. If the child won't stop crying, it's best to leave him alone for a bit (but always keep your eye on the child). Get involved in something else, like sitting on the floor and playing with a toy. Let a little time go by. Soon, you'll probably find the tears have stopped and the child is curious about what you're doing.

Remember, it's important not to lie to the child by saying things like, "Mommy and Daddy will be right back." You want to establish trust, and children can sense when you're not telling the truth.

YOU'RE ON YOUR OWN

The time comes when the parents are gone and you're left with the children. Now what? If you've asked the parents a lot of questions before they left, you have most of the answers you need. And now you'll get a chance to put them into action.

SMART SITTER TIP #6
YOUR BAG OF TRICKS

Put together a tote bag filled with goodies to amuse and entertain the children. Your bag of tricks is especially handy in those first few tense moments when you meet new children. Or, when they've played with all their own toys and are starting to get bored, pull out something fun and new from your bag. Kids love it! You don't have to spend a lot of money. As a matter of fact, you don't have to spend money at all. Use some of these ideas below, or come up with your own creative ideas. Make sure to check the fun and games section beginning on page 31 for more ideas to add to your own bag of tricks.

✔ **coloring books** or a pad of **paper** and a box of **crayons**

✔ **magazines** you can cut up for collages

✔ a **stamp pad, cut-up sponges, water-based paints,** and **paper** to create stationery and cards

✔ **cardboard paper-towel tubes** to create musical horns or tube people (use cut-out faces, arms, legs, and clothes from the magazines)

✔ **glue** for any of the projects above

✔ **tin pie plates** to make cymbals

✔ an **oatmeal box** (with lid) for a drum

✔ **books** from the library (check out pages 43–44 for some children's favorites)

- **First things first.** As soon as the parents leave, make sure you lock the door. Go through the house to make sure all other doors and windows are locked. You may also want to draw the drapes. This may seem overly careful, but a smart sitter is always cautious.

- **When someone calls.** If the parents are expecting any special phone calls, they'll tell you beforehand. If they haven't left any special instructions, never give out any information when you answer a phone. It's best to say, *"Mrs. Johnson is busy and can't come to the phone, but I'll take your name and number so she can get back to you."* Don't let anyone know that you are the babysitter home alone with the children. If you get an obscene phone call, just hang up immediately. Tell the parents about the call when they get home.

- **When someone's at the door.** *Always* use the peephole in the door to see who the visitor is. If there is no way to see who is at the door, then don't open it—ever! It's always better to be safe. As a general rule, you should never let anyone inside whom you do not know. If a delivery person has a package for the parents, he won't mind leaving it at the front door. Leave the package there until the parents get home. If he needs the package signed for, ask him to come back the following day. Remember to tell the parents when they get home.

If neighbors or friends of the parents drop by, they will understand if you don't let them in. And a door-to-door salesman will always come back when the parents are home. Don't even open the door for someone saying they need help. Take their name and information and say you'll call a tow truck or the police while they wait outside. Remember, if you ever get spooked—either by someone at the door or on the phone—call your family or another adult. Sometimes just hearing a calm, familiar voice can soothe your rattled nerves.

- **If your friend comes over.** Sometimes it will be okay with the family to have one of your friends visit. Most of the time it's not a good idea. *Always* check ahead of time with the parents. The family you're sitting for may not like the idea of a friend over to distract you from your main responsibility— their children. Let your friends know ahead of time if they should *not* drop by.

- **Calling friends.** The same rules apply to talking to friends on the phone. Even after the kids are in bed, resist the urge to spend your "free" time on the phone. It's fine to make short calls, or even check in with your family. But you never know when the parents might be calling to check on things or to let you know of a problem. Imagine how embarrassed you'd be if the operator had to break into your conversation with your friend with an emergency call from the parents! It could cost you future jobs with that family.

- **Television and music.** Every family has different rules about watching television. Some parents might let their children have unlimited television privileges, while others might closely monitor and control their children's viewing. Make sure you find out what the children can watch, if anything. Once the kids are safely in bed and sleeping, it's okay to watch television or listen to some music—as long as you've gotten the parents' okay ahead of time. Keep in mind, you're in someone else's home, so follow their rules. Bring your own CDs and cassettes so you don't have to use the family's. Remember, too, it's very important to keep the volume low enough so you can hear the children if they need you or if the baby starts to cry.

- **Smoking and drinking.** Smoking cigarettes and drinking alcohol are absolutely *not* allowed. Being responsible for someone's children can make you feel very grown-up, so remember to make grown-up choices. Smoking and drinking can have dangerous consequences.

- **The family pet.** Remember to find out the rules and routines for the family's pet, too. Is the animal allowed in the house, or does it stay outside? Will you have to feed it? If you feel uncomfort-  able with the pet, or if you have an allergy, ask the family to put it outside or in another room.

- **Dangers lurk everywhere.** Sometimes you'll feel as if you never say anything to a child but "no." Unfortunately, infants, toddlers, and even older children are not aware of things that can cause them harm. So it's crucial to stay alert. Here are some potential dangers to keep them away from— some you may have already thought of, and others you may not be aware of:

WHAT SMART SITTERS SAY

"I don't let my kids watch scary movies anymore when I babysit. Once when I was sitting with this eight-year-old down the street, we watched one of the Nightmare on Elm Street movies. After the movie we both kept hearing noises and seeing things in the shadows. I'll never do that again! Ever!"

Jackie, age 14, Syracuse, New York

✔ **Cleaning supplies:** Parents usually have these items put in a safe place. But if someone has accidentally left a bottle on the counter, put it somewhere out of a child's reach.

✔ **Cords:** Watch out for cords from drapes and mini-blinds. Children can get tangled in them and choke themselves.

✔ **Doors and windows:** Children can hurt themselves falling out of an open window without guards on it, even on the ground floor. And they can easily slip out an open door when your back is turned, then wander into the street. Keep all doors locked and close all unguarded windows.

✔ **Electrical outlets:** Children can be shocked if they poke their fingers, tongues, or other objects into an electrical socket. If there are any exposed wires around electrical outlets, keep the children away from those areas.

✔ **Fans:** Don't let children stick their fingers—or any other objects—into a fan.

✔ **Fireplaces:** Watch babies and toddlers around fireplaces. Fires should never be lit while you're sitting, but even when it's cold, the fireplace may be filled with ash that could be harmful to children.

✔ **Guns:** *Never* touch a gun. If you see one left out, always assume it's loaded. Immediately call an adult to remove it, and keep the children out of the room where it is kept.

✔ **Pools:** If you're sitting at a house with a pool, make sure all access to it is blocked. The doors leading to it should be locked, as well as the fence that surrounds the pool, if there's one. Remember, NEVER leave a child unattended near water—not even near a shallow wading pool or a bucket of water.

✔ **Stairs:** Don't allow children to crawl on stairs. And always hold a toddler's hand when walking up or down. Remember to keep babies far away from staircases.

✔ **Telephone:** Children can become tangled in a telephone cord. And playing with the phone could lead to it being disabled so you couldn't make a call in case of an emergency. The telephone is not a toy and it should be kept out of the reach of young children.

✔ **Tools:** Tools are usually sharp, heavy, and dangerous. Keep children away from tools of any kind (unless they are the child's own play tools).

"ROCK"-A-BYE, BABY

Imagine babysitting for your favorite rock star's child. For some, that's no dream. Traveling in a customized tour bus and having backstage access are just a couple of the perks waiting for backstage babysitters like Maurice. Maurice is a twenty-six-year-old carpenter who now keeps tabs on little Coco Gordon-Moore, the daughter of Sonic Youth's Kim Gordon and Thurston Moore. Maurice didn't set out to be a babysitter. He fell into the situation when he met Gordon and Moore while selling T-shirts at a Sonic Youth concert. Maurice is low-key about taking care of a famous couple's baby. But fame has rubbed off just a little. Maurice has taken a step forward in his own rock career with an appearance in a video by Yo La Tengo.

FUN AND GAMES

• • • • • • • • • • • • • ⚲ • • • • • • • • • • • • •

The greatest part of your job as a babysitter will be keeping the children entertained. Remember when you were little? Playing with your favorite toys was so much fun. And even more enjoyable was having a "new friend" to share toys and learning how to play new games. It's a good idea to go to your babysitting job prepared with lots of ideas for games and activities to keep the kids busy and happy. And you won't have to spend a lot of money, as the following ideas will show. From books to songs to simple crafts, the possibilities are endless. These are just a few samples for fun and games. Remember, a happy child makes a satisfied parent. And a satisfied parent will ask you to babysit again!

LET'S PLAY

If you find the kids are getting restless and bored, there's only one thing to do. Turn off the TV and play! Here are some games and activities that are sure to please and entertain.

Build It with Cards

Ages: six and up

Building cities and palaces out of playing cards can keep kids busy for hours. Building with cards requires dexterity and patience. This is a great activity on a rainy afternoon.

WHAT YOU NEED
• Two or three decks of playing cards (decks that are missing cards are ideal)

WHAT YOU DO

There are no right or wrong ways to build, as long as you can make a building that doesn't topple over. A good base is always the best way to start. It's a good idea to show the child how the cards can be balanced against each other. Experiment with different ways to balance the cards against each other. But be careful—one false move and the elaborately constructed card palace will topple!

WHAT SMART SITTERS SAY

"I'm really good with my yo-yo, so I bring it along when I babysit. The kids like the tricks I do."

Michael, age 14, Phoenix, Arizona

Slap Jack

Ages: five and up

Here's another game to play using cards. Kids love this fast action game because there's something to do with their hands along with the card play. The game works as well with two players as with five or six.

WHAT YOU NEED

- A deck of cards (a standard 52-card deck—no jokers)

WHAT YOU DO

Shuffle the deck and deal *all* the cards to players. Some players may get one more card than others, but that's okay. Players don't look at the cards, but instead make facedown piles.

Players take turns picking up the top card from their pile and flipping it faceup on a pile in the middle of the table. Everyone should watch the cards carefully, because when a jack is placed

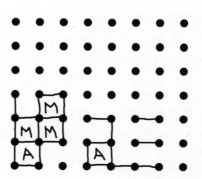

on the pile, the first player to slap his hand on the card wins the pile. These cards are shuffled into the winning player's remaining facedown pile, and the game continues.

If a player mistakenly slaps another card, he must give his top card to the player who put down the slapped card.

Players who have lost all their cards have one chance to stay in the game. If the player with no cards slaps the next jack to come up, he wins the cards in the pile and stays in the game. But if he misses the jack, he's out.

The game continues until one player ends up with all the cards.

Dots and Squares

Ages: seven and up

If the kids you're babysitting love paper and pencil games like tic-tac-toe, they'll flip over this game of dots and lines. This game works best with only two players at a time, so you can be the audience if you're sitting with two kids and they both want to play.

WHAT YOU NEED
- Paper (plain is fine, but lined or graph paper is better)
- Pencils (one for each player)

WHAT YOU DO

On the paper, draw a large rectangle of dots laid out in rows. There should be at least twelve to fifteen rows in each direction.

Each player takes turns drawing lines to connect any two dots, either vertically or horizontally. The object of the game is for one player to complete as many small squares as he can, while preventing his opponent from doing the same thing. Whenever a player sees a place on the game sheet where three sides of a square have been completed, he may draw the fourth side and put his initial in the box. That player earns another turn. If he completes a box on that turn, he can take another turn, and so on until he is unable to complete a box.

When no more lines can be drawn, the player with the most squares filled in and initialed is the winner.

Concentration

Ages: six and up

Matching games have been kid favorites for a long time. Concentration is a classic, played for generations. Not only is this game fun, it tests the alertness and memory of the players.

> ## My Favorite Babysitter
>
> *"Kari is my best babysitter because she always has fun activities planned for my kids when she comes over. They love her!"*
>
> **Jody, mother of two daughters**
> **Miami, Florida**

What You Need
• A deck of cards (you can include the jokers)

What You Do
First, check to make sure every card has a match. Spread all the cards out on a table, facedown. Each player turns over two cards on his turn. If they are the same (such as two red fours, two black queens, etc.), the player keeps them and turns over two more cards. If the cards don't match, turn them back facedown. The trick of the game is to remember the position of the cards to make a match later on. It gets easier as fewer cards are left.

The winner is the player with the most pairs.

For younger kids, you might want to use only half a deck of cards.

FOR KIDDIES UNDER FOUR . . .

Toddlers are always ready to play, but not with any one thing for long. You'll need to have lots of ideas ready to keep a toddler busy. Most toddlers won't play games with lots of rules. Keep playtime simple with some of these ideas:

- Get moving with games like Ring-Around-the-Rosy and London Bridge.

- Toddlers like action toys that let them feel grown-up. Toy sweepers, lawn mowers, wagons, telephones, and dolls are a lot of fun.

- Read a story. Toddlers don't have long attention spans, so get the child involved in the story by asking questions about the pictures and characters. Make sure the book has lots of pictures you can point to.

- Play puppets. Make your puppet with a lunch-sized sack. Use crayons to draw a face on the bottom of the bag.

- Have a stack of fun with building blocks. You'll probably find yourself doing the building while the toddler knocks the blocks down—that's their favorite part!

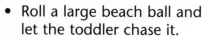

- Roll a large beach ball and let the toddler chase it.

- A large cardboard box can become a house, a spaceship, or race car. Just make sure the toddler can get out easily.

Grandmother's Trunk

Ages: six and up

Here's another memory-testing game. It can be played with two or more players, and since you don't need any materials, it can be played anywhere.

WHAT YOU DO

Each player gets to fill an imaginary "grandmother's trunk"—the trick is the objects must be put in the trunk in alphabetical order. The first player thinks of an object, beginning with the letter *a*, such as an aardvark, and says, "I put an *aardvark* in Grandmother's trunk." Then Player Two thinks of another object that begins with the letter *b*, a banana, for instance. Player Two says, "I put an *aardvark* and a *banana* in Grandmother's trunk." The goal is to remember everything that's gone into the trunk, repeat it in the order it was given, and add a new object.

The fun in this game is to see how many objects you can "put" in the trunk. If a player forgets an item or gets the order wrong, he or she is out. Last player in the game wins.

GET CREATIVE!

Kids love doing arts and crafts. But remember always to get the parents' permission before doing any craft activities. Explain what you plan to do and if you will need to use any of their supplies. And don't forget to clean up when you're finished!

Playtime Dough

Ages: four and up

Make up a batch of playtime dough and mold and shape all kinds of fun things—from animals to out-of-this-world creatures. Just remember, don't let the kids eat the dough.

WHAT YOU NEED

- 2 cups flour
- 1 cup salt
- ¾ cup water

- Few drops of food coloring
- 2 tablespoons cooking oil

WHAT YOU DO

Depending on the ages of the children, you may want to allow them to mix up the dough. First, combine the flour and salt in a large bowl. (If you're bringing the supplies, you can do this at home and put it in a plastic bag.) Then, in a separate bowl, mix a little food coloring and the water. Then add the oil. Slowly stir the water mixture into the dry ingredients. Use your fingers to mix it all together. As you continue mixing (or kneading), the dough will become soft and pliable.

Mold and sculpt the dough into shapes. If the kids want to keep their sculptures, set them in an area to air-dry. Let the parents know it takes a few days. Then the next time you babysit, you can help the kids paint the shapes with poster or acrylic paints!

If you have any dough left over, you may want to store it in a plastic bag or container in the refrigerator.

WHAT SMART SITTERS SAY

"When I take care of babies I have this bag full of scrap material from my mom's sewing basket. The material has to have texture, like terry cloth and velvet. Babies like the feel of it."

Yolanda, age 14, Norfolk, Virginia

Blobs of Art

Ages: four and up

You never know what kind of masterpiece will be created with this technique. But whatever the outcome, you'll be sure to have loads of fun.

WHAT YOU NEED

- Newspaper
- Paper (typing or craft paper)
- 3 to 5 small containers of poster paint in different colors
- Paintbrushes or Popsicle sticks for each color of paint

WHAT YOU DO

Cover your work area with newspaper and make sure the kids are wearing clothes they can get dirty (or put old paint shirts on them). Fold a piece of paper in half, then unfold. Dip into the paint with your paintbrush or Popsicle sticks. Drop a few small blobs of paint on one half of the paper.

Fold the paper again. Press down lightly over the whole surface. Now open it and look at your work of art.

Let each child name her creation, then you can write the name at the bottom of the picture.

Put on a Shadow Play

Ages: four and up

When you were a kid, you probably made shadow pictures on the wall with your hands. Here's an idea that takes those shadow pictures one step further—shadow puppets. Who needs television when you can make your own shows?

WHAT YOU NEED

- Construction paper
- Animal cookie cutters
- Pencil or crayons
- Tape
- Scissors (make sure younger children use safety scissors)

- Popsicle sticks
- Flashlight

WHAT YOU DO

Place the cookie cutters on the paper and trace around them with the pencil or crayons. Use the scissors to cut out the animal shapes, then tape each one to the end of a Popsicle stick.

Shine the flashlight on the puppets so that they cast shadows on the wall. Act out the child's favorite fairy tale or nursery rhyme. Or reenact a scene from a favorite movie or television show.

Hats Off . . . and On!

Ages: four and up

Everyone loves to wear hats, and children love to make them! With a few simple materials you can help kids make unique homemade headpieces.

WHAT YOU NEED

- Lightweight cardboard
- Construction paper
- Stickers (star-shaped or whatever else you can find)
- Glitter
- Paint (poster or acrylic in different colors)
- Tape
- Craft glue
- Scissors

WHAT YOU DO

Start by making a hat base. Cut the cardboard in long strips, one inch wide. Place one of the strips around the child's head right above his ears (like a headband) to get the right size. Remove it and tape or staple the band together. Use a second cardboard strip to go from the left ear over the top of the child's head to the right ear. Staple or tape the top strip to the headband.

Now cut shapes out of the construction paper. You could cut feather shapes, shell shapes, or abstract shapes. Cut strips of construction paper, half an inch wide. Curl the strips around a pencil. Now tape or glue your various pieces to the two strips that make up the hat. You can also glue or tape strips together to create chains to hang around the hat.

Funny Pictures

Ages: four and up

Here's an activity that creates works of art and uses up those old magazines piling up in the corner of your room. Kids of all ages will get a kick out of the strange and funny pictures they can make.

WHAT YOU NEED
- Old magazines
- Scissors
- White glue

WHAT YOU DO

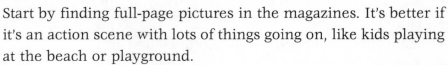

Start by finding full-page pictures in the magazines. It's better if it's an action scene with lots of things going on, like kids playing at the beach or playground.

Then cut out small pictures and objects from the rest of the magazine. Glue these pieces to the big picture. The objects can add to the story of the original picture, or make it weird and silly. Imagine adding a dog's head to a person's body. Or having a giant soda pop can hovering over the scene like a flying saucer. For that matter, why not make the soda pop can a flying saucer, with strange little characters poking their heads out of the windows! The possibilities are unlimited and amazing!

In every craft you and the kids make, don't forget to let the children know how wonderful their projects are. Make a big deal of showing their masterpieces to the parents when they get home.

BABY PLAY

If you think babies just sleep and eat, you're in for a surprise—a delightful one. Babies change and develop more in their first year than at any other time. It's true that newborns don't require a whole lot of play. A few minutes of playing with a soft toy or looking at a mobile is all they can handle at one time. At about three months old, babies are much more aware of the world around them. And by six months, babies can laugh and play peekaboo games. As the one-year mark approaches, babies begin crawling and walking. At this stage they are into everything, so stay alert.

LET'S SING

Preschool- and kindergarten-age kids love to sing, especially when they can act out the actions that tell a story. The following singing games have been handed down from generation to generation, and they're still favorites with kids today.

"Itsy-Bitsy Spider"

WORDS	ACTIONS
1. The itsy-bitsy spider went up the waterspout.	Touch the forefinger of one hand to the thumb of the other and then turn the hands so the other thumb and forefinger touch. Do this several times, raising hands higher and higher.
2. Down came the rain, and washed the spider out.	Shake your hands and wiggle fingers, moving them lower with each shake.
3. Out came the sun, and dried up all the rain.	Make a large circular motion with arms over your head.
4. And the itsy-bitsy spider went up the spout again.	Repeat the action for first line.

"If You're Happy"

WORDS	ACTIONS
If you're happy and you know it, clap your hands. (clap, clap)	At the end of the first, second, and fourth lines, clap your hands twice. Do it again, but each time use a different action, such as:
If you're happy and you know it, clap your hands. (clap, clap)	
If you're happy and you know it, then your life will surely show it.	"Stamp your feet." "Nod your head." "Blink your eyes."
If you're happy and you know it, clap your hands. (clap, clap)	"Turn around and wave good-bye."

"Where Is Thumbkin?"

WORDS	ACTIONS
Where is Thumbkin? Where is Thumbkin?	Both hands are hidden behind singer's back.
Here I am. Here I am.	Right hand is brought out in front, thumb pointing up. Left hand does the same.
How are you today, sir?	Right thumb "bows" four times.
Very well, I thank you.	Left thumb does the same.
Run away. Run away.	Right hand disappears behind back. So does the left.

BUDDING BOOKWORMS!

Children love books. Even if they haven't learned how to read yet, little kids love to be read to. And if they are starting to read, have them read to you so they can practice their skills. You can make reading a special treat when you babysit. Remember to bring two or three books to share. You can find everything at the library. If you're not sure what is age-appropriate for the child you are babysitting, ask the librarian for suggestions. The best way to find books is to pick out those that you loved when you were a kid. You may also want to check with the children's librarian for a list of local favorites. In the meantime, try one of the following books:

Preschool to Seven Years Old

- *The Real Mother Goose* (Rand McNally)
- *A Child's Garden of Verses* by Robert Louis Stevenson (Scribner's)

- *The Tale of Peter Rabbit* by Beatrix Potter (Warne)
- *Just So Stories* by Rudyard Kipling (Peter Bedrick Books)
- *The Velveteen Rabbit* by Margery Williams (Knopf)
- *The Cat in the Hat* by Dr. Seuss (Random House)

For older kids, you may want to pick books that you can read a chapter at a time. Then, each time you babysit, you can read another section.

Eight- to Eleven-year-olds

- *Little House on the Prairie* by Laura Ingalls Wilder (HarperCollins)
- *Five Children and It* by E. Nesbit (Picture Book Studio)
- *Stuart Little* by E. B. White (HarperCollins)
- *Charlotte's Web* by E. B. White (HarperCollins)
- *James and the Giant Peach* by Roald Dahl (Knopf)
- *The Black Stallion* by Walter Farley (Random House)

BABYSITTING MANIA!

The Baby-Sitters Club is one of the hottest and biggest-selling series of books for girls between the ages of eight and twelve. Ann Martin is the creator and writer of those books. She has years of experience that she draws on for ideas. Not only is she a former babysitter, she also has fond memories of being a child. Ann says her favorite babysitter when she was a kid was a teenage boy. Why? Because he taught her how to burp! One of the most bizarre stories she remembers from her babysitting days was a "snake-sitting" episode. She was taking care of a neighbor's pet snake. It should have been a simple job—feed the snake and make sure it didn't get out of its tank. Unfortunately, something happened. The snake didn't make it through the weekend. To this day, Ann still doesn't know why the snake died.

THE INSIDE SCOOP ON FEEDING & BEDTIME

There's a lot involved when taking care of children. You already know how important it is to keep them safe and entertained. Now it's time for the other necessities. Sometimes during your babysitting career you'll be required to feed the children in your care, as well as put them to bed. And if you're sitting for babies and toddlers, you'll probably be changing diapers, too. The following ideas should help make these tasks less daunting and more pleasant for you and for the child you're babysitting.

WHEN IT'S FEEDING TIME

Children are often very specific about what they like to eat. Some kids may only want to eat one kind of food, while others will avoid anything resembling a vegetable. As the babysitter, you don't have to worry about setting their eating patterns for life. Always follow the parents' instructions. They may leave you with specific menus to feed the kids, or give you a choice of foods.

The most important thing you need to know is if a child has any dietary restrictions. You may want to ask the parent if the child is allergic to any foods, such as nuts or milk. Both of these foods can cause severe reactions.

Remember to check with parents first before bringing treats for the children. You may think it's a great way to break the ice with the kids, but the parents may have rules about treats and snacks. It's always best to ask first.

Don't worry if the kids don't eat much. It's amazing, but kids usually get just the right amount of food their bodies need.

When you're preparing food, remember always to wash your hands with soap first. Rinsing with water only is not enough to kill the germs that spread illnesses. Make sure the children wash their hands before they eat as well.

Feeding Basics for Babies

If you feel the least bit nervous, relax. Babies have great radar and can pick up on your tenseness. The parents will tell you when and what to feed the baby. It's a good idea to have them teach you the proper feeding techniques as well. Make sure you feel prepared and confident before you begin doing this on your own. If the baby isn't sitting up yet, you may have to hold the baby while feeding, unless there is a special rocking chair that the parents use. More feeding facts:

- Between the ages of four to six months (and sometimes before), the baby will start on solid foods. This is usually cereal mixed with formula, juice, water, or canned baby foods. You'll probably use a small, soft spoon to feed the baby. Don't give the baby too much at one time. It's a slow process. Babies tend to spit out as much as they take in. Keep a washcloth handy.

- If the baby is in a highchair, make sure to use the straps so he won't slide out of the seat. And as he gets a little older and is able to hold the spoon, put newspaper or a dishtowel down on the floor. At this age, flying food is a "natural" part of the whole eating experience.

If the baby is bottle-feeding only, read up on these bottle basics:

- The parents will probably leave you sterilized bottles. If not, ask them to show you how they do it. Every family has their own way of doing things, and you'll want to follow their routines.

- The formula may need to be made. Sometimes that's as easy as pouring a ready-mixed formula into a bottle. Other times, it means mixing the formula—either a powder or a liquid—with water or juice.

- You'll need to warm the bottle before feeding the baby. The easiest way is to hold the bottle under hot running water. Shake the bottle to mix the formula and give it an even, warm temperature. Then test a couple of drops on the inside of your wrist. If it's too hot for you, it's too hot for the baby. Most baby-care experts caution against warming the bottle in the microwave. Its uneven heating tends to leave pockets of scalding liquid that burn a baby's mouth.

- Put a bib on the baby. Baby formulas leave stains that are hard to get out. You may want to throw a clean towel over your shoulder as well (especially useful when you have to burp the baby).

- Hold the baby in the crook of your arm. The bottle should be at an angle so the nipple is full of milk. You want the baby to get liquid, not air.

- Never prop up the bottle on a pillow in the crib and leave the baby alone.

- At least once during the feeding, burp the baby. You'll do it at the end of the feeding as well. This helps the baby get rid of some of the air he's taken in. Too much air can lead to bellyaches. (Not burping is often painful for a little baby.) Hold the baby against your shoulder and gently rub and pat his back until he burps. Another way is to lay the baby on his belly on your lap with your hand underneath him while you use the other hand to rub his back.

WHAT SMART SITTERS SAY

"The best time is when I'm feeding the baby in the rocking chair. It's such a quiet and special moment between us."

Nicole, age 14, Berkeley, California

Feeding Basics for Toddlers

Just because toddlers can feed themselves doesn't make the experience any less challenging. Check with parents for times of meals and snacks. Ask about amounts the child usually eats, bibs, special cups, plates, and spoons. Here are a few helpful hints to keep in mind.

- You want to completely prepare the meal before putting a child in a highchair.

- Be careful about leaving dangerous objects out for toddlers to grab. That means keeping knives and hot dishes out of reach. Also, turn the handles of pots to a position where children cannot grab them.

- If the toddler is in a highchair, make sure to use the straps. Toddlers can wiggle around and fall out of the highchair as easily as a baby.

- Generally, it's not a good idea to mix eating time with playtime. Too much laughing and giggling can cause a child to choke.

- Cut the toddler's food into small pieces—about the size of the tip of your pinkie finger.

- If she is able, let the toddler feed herself.

- Don't worry if she doesn't eat all her food.

- Watch out for flying food. It might be safer to keep the glass of milk or juice off the highchair tray. Give it back to the toddler when she's ready to take a sip.

- You might want to put something under the highchair, like a towel, to catch dropped food. Also, keep that napkin or washcloth handy.

- Don't feed toddlers nuts, popcorn, grapes, or hard candy. These items can get lodged in their throats, causing them to choke.

Feeding Basics for Older Children

The job of feeding does get easier with older children. Your biggest job will be deciding what to feed them and cleaning up afterward. Older kids can be great helpers if you give them a chance. Here are tips to help you:

- Get older kids involved by giving them a job to do, like setting the table.

- Don't allow any horsing around. An older child can choke as easily as an infant or toddler.

SMART SITTER TIP #7
HEALTHY SNACKS

If parents have given you permission to give their children a snack but no specific guidelines—think healthy! Low-fat and good-for-you don't have to be bad words to kids. It's a good idea to get permission from the parent before using any kitchen appliances, especially the electric ones. Be creative and make the snacks kid-appealing. Try cutting up a few pieces of vegetables and fruits and arrange them on plates in the shape of faces, cars, or boats. Here are a few more ideas you might want to try:

MERRY BERRY DIP

In a blender, process 8 ounces of fresh or frozen strawberries with 4 ounces of softened cream cheese, ¼ cup of reduced fat sour cream (or yogurt), and 1 tablespoon of sugar. Dip in pieces of fresh fruit (apples, strawberries, or peaches) for a fruit snack. This makes six ¼-cup servings.

SAFARI SANDWICHES

Mix ½ cup of reduced-fat cream cheese with ¼ cup of chopped, unpeeled apple, 1 teaspoon of sugar, and ⅛ teaspoon of cinnamon. Toast four slices of raisin bread, then use animal cookie cutters to cut out shapes. Spread the cream cheese mixture on toasted bread shapes. This makes four servings.

TACO PAPO

In a large bowl, spray 4 cups of air-popped popcorn with butter-flavored, nonstick cooking spray. Mix ½ teaspoon of chili powder with ¼ teaspoon of salt and ¼ teaspoon of garlic powder. Sprinkle this mixture over the popcorn and mix lightly to evenly coat. This makes four 1-cup servings.

PURPLE COW SHAKE

In a blender, process 3 cups of nonfat frozen vanilla yogurt with 1 cup of 2% low-fat milk, ½ cup thawed frozen grape juice concentrate (undiluted), and 1½ teaspoons lemon juice. This makes four 1-cup servings.

What to Make

A babysitting job isn't the time to practice your cooking skills. If the parents haven't made specific plans for what to feed the kids, keep it simple and healthy. Add vegetable sticks and fruit to round out the meal. Simple ideas include:

✔ cereal
✔ sandwiches
✔ scrambled eggs
✔ hot dogs
✔ canned foods

IT'S BEDTIME

Up to this point, everything has been pretty much a snap. Right? Well, bedtime may be a little different. It means the end of playtime. And almost no child likes that! Find out from the parents if there are any bedtime rituals. Does the child have to sleep with a special stuffed toy or blanket? Is a night-light left on, and

---

AVOID THE BATH-TIME BLUES

It's generally a good idea to avoid giving baths to children. There are so many things that can go wrong. For this reason, you should tell the parents that you would feel more comfortable if they would give their child a bath before you take over. You'll find parents will respect your decision, and will most likely be relieved that you're putting their children's safety first.

is the bedroom door open or shut? You'll use the same technique for naptime as well. Try some of these bedtime ideas to help keep the "good" in good night!

For Babies

Find out the baby's sleeping position. If in doubt, always put babies on their backs. Make sure there are no small objects in the crib. Older brothers and sisters are notorious for accidentally dropping small toys in the baby's crib. The parents should let you know if the baby uses a pacifier. Always make sure the rails are up and locked into place.

For Older Kids

- **Give a warning.** About twenty minutes or so before bedtime, let toddlers and older children know that bedtime will soon be at hand.

- **Quiet time.** If the child has been playing hard right before bedtime, no amount of coaxing will get him to sleep. Plan some quiet time fifteen to twenty minutes before bed. Curl up on the sofa and read a book or tell a favorite story.

- **Follow the routines.** All children have regular routines they like to follow. Ask the child what his is and get him to show you. It'll get him involved with his own bedtime.

- **Be firm.** Children will test their limits. Be prepared for "another glass of water" or "one more story" or "a hug, *pleeeze!*" The only thing to do is take him back to bed, again and again if you have to. After a while, the child will know you mean business and give up.

- **Fears.** Some children wake up with nightmares and bad dreams. If this happens, the best thing you can do is be there for the child. Sometimes just sitting nearby will reassure the child that everything is okay. A hug may work even better.

WHAT SMART SITTERS SAY

"I read stories to the kids at bedtime. Sometimes it's the same story, over and over again. Kids like to hear a story they know."

Mallory, age 13, Toledo, Ohio

TIME FOR A CHANGE

One of the least favorite jobs of babysitting is changing diapers and helping toddlers "use the potty." Keep in mind it's a natural function. Don't make a big deal out of it. And don't make the child feel this is a yucky thing. Remember to smile.

Changing a Diaper

There are probably as many ways to diaper a baby as there are babies. Disposable or cloth diapers? Pins or tape? Lotion or ointment? Find out where the clean and dirty diapers are kept and where the baby is usually changed (changing table or bed). It is a good idea to watch the parents change the baby you will be sitting for. And remember these guidelines:

- *Never* leave a baby alone on a changing table.

- Before you take the soiled diaper off, look carefully at how it was put on by the parent.

- Wash the baby's bottom each time you change her. Use a baby wipe or clean, soapy cloth. Pat her (don't rub) with a soft towel.

- Apply the lotion or ointment the parents have given you.

- Hold the baby's feet with one hand and slide the diaper under her bottom with the other hand.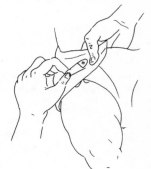

- If you're using cloth diapers and pins, pull the side of the diaper out with two fingers so you create a buffer between the pin and the baby's skin.

- If you are using disposable diapers, tape the two sides tightly to avoid leaks. (Of course, be careful not to fasten *too* tight!)

- Never put pins, lotions, or soiled diapers within reach of the baby.

- If you're changing a boy baby, lay a loose diaper over his genitals or you might get hit by an accidental spray. (Yes, it happens all the time!)

- Dispose of the diapers as the parents have instructed.

- Always wash your hands after you've changed the baby.

Toileting a Toddler

Generally, toilet training starts around two years old. As a babysitter, you should not be expected to do the training, only to reinforce what the parents have already started. What you need to know is if the toddler is in training. Find out from the parents what the procedure is. You may have to encourage him to take time out from playing to go to the bathroom. Will the toddler tell you? Or is it a facial expression that clues the parents to the necessity? Does the toddler use the regular toilet or a special potty seat or chair? Does the child need any help? You might have to help the child unfasten clothes, or you might be required to help with wiping. Congratulate the child when he does a good job. Always make sure the child washes his hands, and you should as well, if you've helped.

Remember to periodically ask toddlers if they have to go to the bathroom, because most children don't always make announcements! And always have toddlers go to the bathroom before going to bed. This could help avoid nighttime accidents.

WHAT SMART SITTERS SAY

"The little boy I'm babysitting for is just starting potty training. He's so proud of himself when he goes. It's really cute."

Emily, age 13, Temecula, California

OTHER MESSES THAT ARE BOUND TO HAPPEN

It's inevitable: children make messes. Your job shouldn't be to clean the house, but when accidents occur you need to deal with them.

Vomit and Spit-up

It's pretty normal for a baby to spit up or even vomit. It might be that the contents of his tummy are unsettled, or the baby's been jostled and bounced a bit too much. Older children can have problems, too—especially if they've been crying too hard, or are coming down with an illness.

- Wipe up the mess with paper towels. Then check the cleaning supplies for an antibacterial cleanser. If that's not available, dilute a small amount of baking soda in warm water and wipe up with a sponge. Baking soda helps remove the smell. Make sure to keep the child away from the cleaning supply bottles.

- Rinse clothing or bed linens under cold water. Then soak the clothing in a solution of ¼ cup of baking soda and 1 gallon of warm water.

- Clean furniture or carpeting as best you can with paper towels and wipe with the soda-and-water solution.

- Tell the parents about the incident. They may have to follow up with special cleaning methods in those areas.

Accidental Urination and Bowel Movements

Sometimes you'll find that a child just can't make it to the bathroom. Or maybe he'll come down with diarrhea. Try not to get upset. Remember, the child did not do it on purpose. Tell him that it's okay, and that everyone has accidents.

- Take off the soiled clothing. Clean the child up and put on fresh clothing right away.

- Clean up any solids with paper towels or toilet paper and dispose of them in the toilet or outside garbage.

- Blot up liquids on furniture and carpets with a paper towel. Then use a sponge to wash the area down with cold water.

- Make sure to tell the parents when they arrive home.

When Something Breaks

It happens. Something is pulled down from a shelf or a ball hits the window. The first thing you need to do is keep the child away from sharp objects. Put a  baby in his crib or infant seat. Distract a toddler or older child with a video or a book while you take care of it.

- Clean up the mess, but be careful not to cut yourself on broken glass or sharp fragments.

- Sweep or vacuum the area carefully.

- Make sure to tell the parents.

- Most importantly, don't get upset with the child. Stay calm and relaxed. Some children will feel embarrassed or ashamed. It's up to you to make them feel better.

EXPECT THE UNEXPECTED

• • • • • • • • • • • • • • •   🔔   • • • • • • • • • • • • • •

Most of the time, your babysitting jobs will be problem-free. But as every good babysitter will tell you, anything can happen. As a babysitter, the most important part of your job is to always be prepared.

TEARS AND FEARS

You can avoid most tearful problems by staying involved with the children. But sometimes a child cries. He might be scared, sick, angry, or hurt. Whatever the reason, the child needs your attention immediately.

- **Determine the problem.** First, you must stay calm. Don't panic. And don't yell. That's a sure way to make a child cry harder and longer. Use a calm, gentle approach. With a soothing voice, try to calm the child down. Listen to how the child is crying. Is it an "owie" or "Mommy, come back" that has him sobbing?

- **What to do.** If it's an "owie" that has the child upset, check him from head to toe for injuries. Try to keep the child from moving, so that any injuries will not be made worse. A scraped knee will be obvious, but a bitten tongue or even a broken bone may not be. If the problem isn't an "owie," then all that might be needed is a little TLC (tender loving care). A kiss and a hug may be just the right medicine to relax and soothe a child.

- **When tears become a temper tantrum.** Sometimes crying will go on until it becomes a temper tantrum. That's when the crying suddenly includes kicking, screaming, yelling, and hitting. It may seem the more you try to stop the crying, the worse the tantrum can get. The most important thing for you to do is remain calm. Your main goal is to prevent the child from hurting himself or others. While it may be difficult, try to ignore the tantrum. Look as if you are doing something else, but always keep the child in sight. Once the tantrum reaches its end, offer a distraction—a game, a walk around the house, or a toy.

  Any time you think a child has cried continuously for too long, call the parents.

- **Breath holders.** What happens if you babysit a child who holds his breath as a sign of anger or frustration? First, relax—his head will not explode. The child's face will become pale, or sometimes red or blue. He might pass out briefly and then begin breathing again on his own. You won't have to begin rescue breath as long as you can see the child breathing. The best thing to do is to avoid the problem in the first place. If you see the child beginning to get frustrated, distract him with a new activity.

- **Quiet time.** When the child seems to be getting out of hand, quiet time may be the answer. Just put the child in a chair to sit and settle down. As a rule of thumb, time-outs should be one minute for every year of age. Remember, never spank a child or call her names.

- **Babies cry for a reason.** Babies can't tell you what's wrong, but if they cry, you should assume there is a problem. It might simply be because they're wet, hurt, bored, or tired. They have different cries that mean different things. Some babies cry because of colic. These babies will seem to be in great pain. Their tummies become hard and swollen and they sometimes stiffen their legs. Medical experts believe colic is caused by sharp pains in the intestine. The problem for you is there's not much you can do to help the baby. The best remedy seems to be holding, rocking, and walking with the baby until the pain passes. If the baby continues to cry, don't hesitate to call the parents.

SMART SITTER TIP #8
SIBLING RIVALRY

Chances are at some point you'll babysit for more than one child. Brother-brother. Sister-sister. Brother-sister. Whatever the combination, more than one child in the family means potential problems with sibling squabbles. If you have a brother or sister, you know all about this. As a sitter who's only with the kids for a few hours, you don't have time to get into permanent solutions. Here are some must-try tips for sparring siblings:

- **Separate the children to opposite sides of the room.** But don't make it a punishment—give them each their own activity to do.

- **Head off an argument before it starts.** You can tell when siblings are starting to get on each other's nerves. Start a new game or activity to distract them from their disagreement.

- **Reward good behavior.** If a dispute is brewing, make them an offer they can't refuse. "Hey, guys, if we can do a puzzle without fighting, I'll read you an extra-long story at bedtime."

WHEN AN EMERGENCY HAPPENS

You will most likely never have a real emergency while you're babysitting. But always go into a job thinking that one might occur. If something does happen, don't panic. It's really important for you to stay calm. It's better to take a few seconds to take a calming breath than to run around in panic and do the wrong thing. Remember, the way you handle an emergency will affect how the child responds. If you act scared, the child might panic. Try to remain calm and matter-of-fact about the situation. Make it a small adventure. If the emergency is an injury or illness, turn to page 65 for specific first aid advice. Otherwise, check out the emergencies listed here and be prepared!

ALWAYS REMEMBER . . . STAY CALM.

Fire

If you discover fire or heavy smoke, get yourself and the child out of the house immediately! Don't try to find out where the fire is coming from or try to put it out. Don't even worry about trying to call the fire department. Forget about coats or shoes. Even if the child is wearing nothing but a diaper, just get the child and leave the house. Go to the nearest neighbor and telephone the fire department from there. Then telephone the parents.

Flood

Unless you live in a coastal area or near a river, you might never think a flood could happen. However, water pipes have been known to leak and sometimes burst. Water on the floor becomes dangerous when it reaches electrical wiring. Or a floor could become weakened by the water and collapse. As with a fire or a gas leak, in the case of a flood it's important to take the child to the nearest neighbor and telephone the fire department.

Gas Leak

If the parents you're sitting for use a gas stove in the kitchen, always check to make sure all the burners are in the "off" position. Escaping gas can be hard to smell if the leak is small. But make no mistake, small or not, a gas leak is very dangerous. Over time it can cause unconsciousness, or, if ignited, an explosion. If you smell gas and cannot immediately find its source to turn it off, get yourself and the child out of the house. Go to the nearest neighbor and have them call the gas company. Someone will be sent at once to check the leak.

Power Failure

If there is a blackout in your neighborhood, don't panic. It might be caused by a storm or an overload on the system, like during the summer when everyone is running their air conditioners. First, reassure the child that everything is all right. Then get out the flashlight. (You should know where that is because it's on the checklist you made before the parents left!) You may want to call the phone company. They'll let you know what area is affected by the blackout and when it should be fixed. Stay inside and settle the child down for a quiet activity, like a picnic in the dark with cookies and a glass of milk. Or tell a favorite story (just nothing scary).

Prowler

When you're in a strange home with a child, it's easy to think every creak and groan is something sinister. Don't worry, it's probably just a bad case of nerves and an active imagination. Even so, always stay alert. If you really think someone is outside, or you see someone at a door or window, call the police at once. Stay calm and make sure you tell them as accurately as possible what you've seen or heard. The police will want to know the address of the house, the phone number, and your name. If you checked the windows and doors when the parents first left, you'll be okay until the police come. Remember to never open the door to someone you don't know. Even the police. Ask for identification first and check it through the peephole or a window. The same thing goes if you start getting nuisance phone calls. Call the police. If a prowler does break in, cooperate with him. The household possessions are not important. But the children's safety—and yours—is!

Severe Weather

If you live in areas where severe weather occurs (earthquakes, tornadoes, and hurricanes), make sure you know the basics of what to do. Check with the family for their emergency plans. During an emergency it's easy to be confused in a strange house.

Strangers

If a stranger (or someone the children do not know) approaches while you're playing outdoors, go inside immediately and lock the doors. If the person doesn't leave, call the police and the parents.

CALLING FOR EMERGENCY HELP

When an emergency happens, you have to be ready to call for help. That usually means calling 911. Most communities have one central emergency number to route calls to the police and fire departments and paramedics. If you're not sure if there is a 911 service in your area—or you're babysitting in a community you're unfamiliar with—look in the front of the phone book.

This should be part of your overall checklist of things to do as soon as you arrive at the house. Remember, don't wait for an emergency to happen, be prepared. If you find you have to call for emergency help, here are some helpful guides to make sure you give all the vital information:

1. State the problem. Try to be as specific as possible (for example, "A child, age four, has fallen off a swing and might have a broken arm.").

2. Say that you are the child's sitter.

3. Give the exact address and telephone number of your location.

4. Give both your name and the family's name.

5. Do not end the conversation yourself. Wait until the emergency operator tells you to hang up.

BACKUP ADULTS

A backup adult is a responsible adult nearby whom you can call, other than the child's parents. You might feel the need for some advice on how to settle down a rambunctious child, or someone to assist you if an actual emergency happens. The backup adult is most important to give you some peace of mind. You should have a list of adults, but the parents of the child you're sitting for may have their own list as well. These numbers can be added to your emergency card. The backup adult could be a neighbor, grandparent, friend, or relative. Make sure all phone numbers for backup adults are kept in a visible place, like by the phone or on the refrigerator.

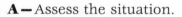

Any time you make an emergency call, follow it up with a phone call to the parents. Let them know where you are (if you've had to call from a neighbor's house or the hospital).

FIRST AID ADVICE

Bumps, bruises, and scratches are bound to happen. Most of the time, they won't be too serious. However, you should have training beforehand, such as with special babysitting or first aid classes in your community. Take a look at these common childhood mishaps and, in addition to what you learn in the first aid courses, follow these ABCs of treatment:

A — Assess the situation.
B — Begin treatment.
C — Call for help when needed.

Animal Bites

A — If an unknown or wild animal bit the child, it may have to be tracked down to be sure it's not carrying rabies.
B — Clean the wound with soapy, running water for five minutes. Put on a sterile bandage.
C — Call the parents immediately.

Blisters

A — Don't worry too much about a blister. It's usually best to do nothing at all.
B — Don't try to break the blister. That could lead to infection. Try to keep the child from an activity that might break it open.
C — Make sure the parents know about it when they get home.

Bloody Noses

A—A nosebleed can be caused by a blow or by poking fingers. There are also a number of other medical conditions that can cause a nosebleed.

B—Blood running down a child's face can be scary, but don't panic. Most nosebleeds will stop by themselves. But if the bleeding continues, have the child sit up, hold his head back slightly, and tell him to breathe through his mouth. Don't have him lie down. That might cause the blood to run down into the throat. You might also try applying pressure to the nose. *Gently* grasp the 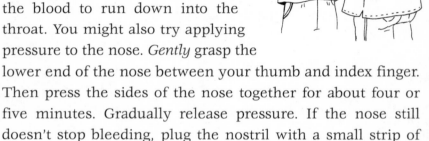 lower end of the nose between your thumb and index finger. Then press the sides of the nose together for about four or five minutes. Gradually release pressure. If the nose still doesn't stop bleeding, plug the nostril with a small strip of sterile gauze rolled up loose (do not use cotton).

C—Call parents if the bleeding does not stop after 15 minutes.

Bruises

A—Check to see that it is a bruise and not a broken bone (see Fractures). A bruise will almost immediately turn purplish.

B—Use an ice pack if the bruise swells. To make your own pack, put ice in a plastic bag. Wrap the bag in a dishtowel and apply to the bump. Leave on for about ten minutes, just long enough to numb the pain. Usually no more than an ice pack and a kiss are needed, and the child will be fine.

C—If the child was hit on the head and she vomits or gets pale, sweaty, or sleepy, it could mean she has a concussion.

Call the parents immediately. Keep in mind a severe bruise might be masking a fracture. If the injury seems serious, the child should see a medical professional right away.

Bug Bites and Bee Stings

A—Mosquito bites can be a problem for little ones. Check with the parents to see if they use insect repellent on the children before they go outside. Find out how much they apply, or read the label directions.

B—If the child is bitten, try to keep her from scratching. This is no easy task. Children don't understand it's bad for them to scratch. All they know is that it itches. Apply a little vinegar to the bite with a cotton ball. It'll take some of the sting away. Some parents use calamine lotion to reduce the itch. For bee stings, gently scrape out the stinger if you can see it. Use an ice pack to reduce swelling. Wash the skin around the sting with soap and water. If the sting starts to itch, use calamine lotion or make a paste of baking soda and a little water.

C—If the child gets pale and sweaty and has trouble breathing, call medical emergency immediately. The child may be having an allergic reaction. Call the parents and have them come home at once.

Burns

A—Determine how severe the burn is. When skin is charred, it's considered a third-degree burn, the most serious. Second-degree burns cause the skin to blister.

B—For minor burns (less than second-degree), put the injured area under cold (but not ice) water. It will take the sting out of the burn. It takes about five to ten minutes to stop the pain. Pat it dry with a clean towel, then leave it alone. Don't apply any creams or medication. But do be sure to let the parents know.

C— For more serious burns, call for emergency help immediately. For third-degree burns, put a clean bed sheet around the child until emergency help arrives. For second-degree burns, place a cool washcloth over the wound until emergency help arrives.

Cuts, Scrapes, and Scratches

A— Check to see how deep the cuts are. If they seem to be minor cuts or scratches, proceed with treatment.

B— The best thing you can do for small cuts and scratches is to wash the injured area with soap and water. You can use an antiseptic ointment, but if you've washed the injury thoroughly, it won't be necessary. Then apply a bandage to keep it clean. Somehow, a bandage always makes the boo-boo better for a child. And don't forget the kiss!

C— If there is a large gash or open wound, call the parents immediately. The child may need stitches. In the meantime, wrap the wound with a clean towel and try to keep the child from moving around.

Fractures

A— It's not always easy to determine if a child has a fracture. It could also be a dislocation of the bone. When a child falls and hurts herself, you must at least consider a fracture as a possibility. What you think is just a sprain may be something more serious. Compare the injured part to the opposite, uninjured part. You may or may not notice a swelling or a deformity of the part that is broken. Do not try to feel it. Do not move the injured part.

B— Keep the child comfortable with blankets and pillows. You want to prevent the child's going into shock.

C— Call 911 immediately. They will send out an ambulance. Then call the parents and let them know.

Poison

A—If you think a child has ingested a poisonous substance, pick up the container and head for the phone immediately to call the Poison Control Center, listed on your emergency card.

B—There are so many different kinds of poisons, remedies, and combinations that it would be impossible to memorize them all, or even look them up in the case of an emergency. Depending on the substance, the Poison Control Center may have you give the child a medicine called syrup of ipecac to induce vomiting. (However, there are some substances ipecac should never be used with, so *always* get instructions from a medical professional first.) Water and milk are also used to dilute the effects of some substances. Don't wait for advice if an irritating substance gets on the skin or in the eyes; flush with lots of water.

C—Call the Poison Control Center, hospital, or doctor immediately. Tell the medical professional what the child took and follow directions.

Splinters

A—They may not seem like serious wounds, but splinters can hurt. And if not taken care of, they can become infected.

B—If you can see a part of the splinter sticking out, remove it. Wash your hands and the area around the splinter. With a pair of tweezers, pull it out.

C—If the splinter is under a fingernail, it's best to leave it until the parents get home.

Sprains

A—Ankle or wrist sprains are the most common. You'll want to be sure there is no breakage (see Fractures).

B—Have the child lie down and elevate the sprained body part. Put an ice pack over the sprained part to keep the swelling down.

C—Call the parents right away. If the sprain stays painful and swollen, they may want the child to be X-rayed when they get home.

Sunburn

A—It's best not to let a child get sunburned in the first place. If you're going to take a child outside on a sunny day, make sure to apply sunscreen beforehand. Make sure he wears a hat, too. But if a child does come in with a red back and arms, proceed with treatment.

B—Apply cool water to the burned areas. Some parents keep aloe vera lotion in the refrigerator to cool burns.

C—If the child gets the chills and a fever, call the parents. A sunburn is still a burn!

Swallowing Small Objects

A—Babies and small children are always putting things in their mouths. That's why it's so important to keep little objects away from them. If the child isn't choking or feeling any discomfort, she may be able to pass the object through her system.

B—If the child is choking, proceed with the Heimlich maneuver on page 72. If not, watch the child carefully for any signs of distress. The parents will have to check the child's bowel movements for a few days to see if the object has passed.

C—Follow proper lifesaving techniques as outlined in the section "A Choking Child" (see page 72) and call for help immediately.

DO YOU KNOW HOW TO SAVE A LIFE?

By now you probably realize there are a lot of things that can go wrong while you're babysitting. That shouldn't scare you, but it should make you aware of just how serious taking care of children is. Two important techniques you should learn are mouth-to-mouth resuscitation if a child stops breathing and the Heimlich maneuver if he is choking. If you think taking a babysitting or life-saving class isn't necessary, think again. You never know when you'll need these skills. A smart sitter knows an emergency can happen anywhere, anytime—while babysitting, at the beach with friends, or even at the dinner table with family!

> **THE FOLLOWING INFORMATION IS NOT INTENDED TO TAKE THE PLACE OF CERTIFIED LIFESAVING TRAINING. IT IS GIVEN ONLY TO FAMILIARIZE YOU WITH THE TECHNIQUES USED AND THE KNOWL-EDGE REQUIRED. IT'S IMPORTANT FOR YOU—AND THE FAMILIES YOU'LL BE SITTING FOR—TO TAKE A LIFESAVING CLASS.**

RESCUE BREATHING

Always remember to remain calm and focused. First call 911. The operator on the line can help you through each of the steps on the following pages. If the child has not breathed for a period of 15 seconds because of choking, near-drowning, electrical shock, or severe head injury, administer mouth-to-mouth breathing imme-diately, following these steps, which were obtained from both the Safe Sitters information packet and from the American Medical Association's Handbook of First Aid and Emergency Care.

1. Gently shake the child and shout, "Are you okay?"

2. If there is no response, call to someone to get help (you may have another child call 911, or call a neighbor).

3. Look, listen, and feel for breathing. Look at the child's chest to see if it's moving.

4. Check the child's mouth for any objects.

5. Tilt the child's head backward to open the airway. (Do this by placing your palm on the child's forehead and the fingers of your other hand under the child's mouth.)

6. Place your mouth over the child's mouth and nose and give two short breaths. Watch for the chest to rise.

7. If the chest doesn't rise, give two more rescue breaths.

8. Look, listen, and feel to see if the child is breathing. If not, resume rescue breathing, with one breath every three seconds.

9. Continue rescue breathing for one minute. Look, listen, and feel to see if the child is breathing. If not, continue rescue breathing until help arrives.

A CHOKING CHILD

A child may choke when an object he's swallowed gets stuck in his throat or windpipe. Act immediately if he is coughing, gagging, has high-pitched breathing, is clutching his neck, or is unable to make a noise when attempting to cough or cry.

1. If the child can speak and is breathing, don't interfere. He may be able to cough out the swallowed object.

2. If the child cannot breathe, stand behind him and place your fist against his stomach, slightly above the navel and below

the ribs and breastbone. Your thumb should be flat against the child's stomach.

3. Hold your fist with your other hand and give four quick, forceful upward thrusts.

4. You may have to repeat this procedure six to ten times.

5. If you cannot dislodge the swallowed object, or the child becomes unconscious, leave the child and call 911 or Emergency Medical Services.

6. Come back to the child. With the child on the floor on his back, give two rescue breaths to open his airway.

7. Straddle the child. Place the heel of one of your hands on the child's stomach—a little above the navel and below the ribs. Put your other hand over the first. Now give four quick, strong forward thrusts. Repeat the cycle of rescue breathing and stomach thrusts until the child is breathing on his own, or until medical help arrives.

THE SMART SITTER

It's a great feeling when you complete your first babysitting job. Along with having done a good job, you'll discover some important things about yourself and about babysitting. First, you will learn you are a responsible, capable person. You will also learn that children need a lot of nurturing, and that there are always new opportunities to improve your babysitting skills.

My Favorite Babysitter

"I had a babysitter who seemed more interested in finishing her homework than taking care of my son. Then I hired Nita. She comes with books and games, and projects the attitude that being with Mason is the greatest thing in the world."

Tina, mother of one boy
Ft. Collins, Colorado

BE SAFE

Your personal safety is just as important as that of the children you watch. You'd never think of letting the child you're responsible for walk into a busy street, right? That would be dangerous. But it's just as dangerous when you don't take your own personal safety seriously.

- **At night.** If you want to walk or ride your bike to and from your employer's home, do it only during daylight hours, never after dark.

- **Drinking and driving.** If your employer is supposed to take you home, but you think he's been drinking, call your parents (or another backup adult). Never get into a car with a person who's been drinking.

MEET AN AWARD-WINNING SITTER

Sarah Nutter is fifteen years old. Like a lot of girls her age, she babysits. But this Ames, Iowa, teenager is no ordinary babysitter. Safe Sitter, a national organization that teaches babysitting basics around the country, named Sarah their 1996 Safe Sitter of the Year for saving a toddler's life.

While watching two neighborhood children, Sarah found herself living a babysitter's worst fear. The two children she was sitting for—Jackson, age two, and Sara, age five—were helping to put toys away to get ready for bed. Jackson pulled a bucket of wooden beads down. They picked the beads up, but Jackson must have hidden one in his hand. Sarah didn't know that at the time.

A short time later, Jackson began choking. His face turned red and he was trying to cry or cough, but couldn't. Sarah didn't panic. She got down on her knees and did the Heimlich maneuver at least five times. When Jackson finally started to cry and could breathe again, Sarah fished the bead out of his mouth.

Sarah was worried that Jackson's throat would swell shut from the incident. She called her mother, then the doctor. She didn't stop worrying until the doctor convinced her Jackson was all right.

This was not the first time Sarah had been involved in an emergency situation. When she was seven years old, *she* was the choking child. A piece of hard candy had lodged in her throat and an older friend performed the Heimlich maneuver on her.

Sarah also credits her quick action to a babysitting class she took at a local hospital. Sarah remembered her training from the Safe Sitter program the hospital used. And Safe Sitter remembered her when they gave her their annual award.

In the following interview, Sarah talks about her lifesaving experience and being a babysitter.

Q: *Why didn't you panic when Jackson started to choke?*
A: I think I was so shocked, I didn't even think about what I did. I just did it.

Q: *When you took the babysitting class, did you learn emergency procedures?*
A: We spent a while on first aid procedures and we practiced rescue breathing on mannequins. That helped a lot.

Q: *Do you think that having choked as a child yourself had an effect on your actions?*
A: I think it helped because I knew how scared Jackson was feeling.

Q: *How long have you been babysitting?*
A: About three years.

Q: *Did you start babysitting after you took the class, or had you done some before?*
A: I babysat a couple of times before that. Then my mom thought I should take the class at the hospital.

Q: *Did you think you needed to take the class?*
A: No, I didn't think I really needed to.

Q: *Now what do you think?*
A: I think it's good. It helps you *a lot.* More people should do it. I'd liked it because you learned to take care of the small things.

Q: *What kind of small things?*

A: Like how to take care of cuts and bruises, or what to do if a child falls down.

Q: *How do you get most of your babysitting jobs?*

A: I get a lot through my church. And the people I work for give out my name a lot.

Q: *Does your church have a bulletin board where you can post your name?*

A: No, it's mostly because they know who you are. And that you're around little kids a lot.

Q: *Did you volunteer to help in the church's nursery?*

A: That's what I did for a long time before I actually started babysitting.

Q: *Do your parents screen new families who call you?*

A: They ask me how the people got my name. Usually when someone calls me, they always say how they got my name, anyway. Then my parents take their phone number to make sure they have it. And I always call them right when I get to the new house.

Q: *Do you have a favorite age group you like to sit for?*

A: I usually like kids from about six months to five years old.

Q: *What's the oldest child you've sat for?*

A: About eight years old.

Q: *How often do you babysit?*

A: Usually about twice a week, on weeknights and weekends. I have two families that call me all the time right now.

Q: *Why do you babysit?*

A: I like kids a lot, ever since I was little. You can have fun with them.

Q: *What's the scariest part?*

A: I don't like feeding, because I'm always afraid they'll choke.

Q: *Do you know what you want to do when you finish school?*

A: I want to be a physical therapist for pediatrics because I want to do something with kids. I like kids.

Now you've learned the ins and outs of babysitting—from feeding and safety to loads of tips on playing and having fun with the kids. Remember to tuck this book into your "bag of tricks." You may never have to refer to it, but it's nice to know it's there if you need it!

Once you start babysitting, remember to take a few minutes after each job to think about how it went. What were the best things about that babysitting job? Is there anything you'd do differently the next time? If there is, figure out how you can make the change. If you need more information, talk to your family, friends, or the parents of the children you sit for. Remember, how good a babysitter you are is in direct proportion to how much energy and enthusiasm you put into it.

Good luck and have fun!

THE SMART SITTER'S CHECKLIST

(Make copies or copy the list in your notebook, and fill out a sheet for each new job.)

• •

THINGS TO KNOW BEFORE THEY GO

1. Fill out the emergency card on page 21. Also, ask the parents how they want you to handle an emergency if they can't be reached by phone.

2. Find out what parents expect of you on the following:
    ___ Feeding the kids
    ___ Changing diapers/potty training assistance
    ___ Bedtime rules
    ___ Handling the phone
    ___ Entertainment for kids
    ___ Off-limits areas of the house

3. And don't forget these important questions that may or may not be applicable to your situation:
    ___ Is it okay to watch TV or listen to music at a low level when the kids are in bed?
    ___ Do you have any pets I need to feed or take care of?
    ___ Can the kids be outside?
        Do they need to put on sunscreen?
        Put on bug spray?
    ___ Can they have friends over to the house?
    ___ Can they go over to a friend's house?
    ___ Are the kids allergic to anything or taking any medicine, or do they have an illness I should be aware of?

• •

INDEX